# Missel-Child

Helen Tookey was born near Leicester in 1969. She studied philosophy and English literature at university and has worked in publishing, as a university teacher and as a freelance editor. Her poems have appeared in a variety of magazines and anthologies. In addition to poetry she has published critical work including *Anaïs Nin, Fictionality and Femininity* (Oxford University Press, 2003) and *Malcolm Lowry: From the Mersey to the World* (co-edited with Bryan Biggs; Liverpool University Press, 2009).

HELEN TOOKEY

# Missel–Child

CARCANET

# Acknowledgements

Thanks are due to the editors of the following publications, in which some of these poems previously appeared: *Archipelago*, *Best British Poetry 2013* (Salt, 2013), *The Bow-Wow Shop*, *Kaffeeklatsch*, *New Poetries V* (Carcanet, 2011), *New Walk*, *The North*, *PN Review*, *Poetry Proper*, *Poetry Review*, *Poetry Wales*, *The Reader*, *Stand*. Some of the poems also appeared in the pamphlet *Telling the Fractures* (with photographs by Alan Ward; Axis Projects, 2008).

First published in Great Britain in 2014 by
Carcanet Press Limited
Alliance House
Cross Street
Manchester M2 7AQ

www.carcanet.co.uk

A CIP catalogue record for this book is available from the British Library

ISBN 978 1 84777 218 3

The publisher acknowledges financial assistance from Arts Council England

Supported by
**ARTS COUNCIL
ENGLAND**

Typeset by XL Publishing Services, Exmouth
Printed and bound in England by SRP Ltd, Exeter

# Contents

IV

By sitting upon a hill late in an evening, neere a Wood, in a few nights a fire drake will appeare; marke where it lighteth, and there you shall finde an Oake with Misletoe therein, at the Root whereof there is a Misell-child, whereof many strange things are conceived.

Sir Hugh Plat, *The Garden of Eden*, 1653

I

# Then is it true

*Aber weil Hiersein viel ist, und weil uns scheinbar*
*alles das Hiesige braucht, dieses Schwindende, das*
*seltsam uns angeht…*

Rilke, *Ninth Elegy*

Then is it true, that you also need us?

Look: here, at this angle of land, where riverbank
becomes coast, here is salt ice lying

in the furrows, and there, where water
exchanges with water a mode

of being, river/ocean/river, there
again is ice, thin-skinned and scarcely

bearing, puzzling rocks; and the cold,
to us, is like a new live thing, that stalks

the hollows of our bones. – Look: I am
giving it to you, this fragment; but how,

in your completeness, could you need it?

# At Burscough, Lancashire

Out on the ghost lake, what's lost
is everywhere: murmuring in names
on the map, tasted in salt winds
that scour the topsoil, westerlies
that wrenched out oaks and pines, buried now
in choked black ranks, heads towards the east.
Cloudshadows ripple the grasses as the seines
rippled over the mere by night, fishervoices calling
across dark water. Underfoot, the flatlands'
black coffers lie rich with the drowned.

# Prints

*…within some strata the footprints of the animals, birds and humans
frequenting the coast at that time have been preserved… The females, often
accompanied by children, would appear to have been mainly occupied with
gathering food, e.g. shrimps, razor shells and other seafood. At one site there
was a wild confusion of children's footprints as though they had been
mudlarking…*

Gordon Roberts, 'The Lost World of Formby Point'

I

Patience you need and a strong back for digging
razor-clams, wheedling them up with salt and
tugging them out, blind snouts curling. Bored, the
children play catch-me-if-you-can, eeling
from each other's muddy hands, filthy and
shrieking with laughter. Minding the tide and
uncertain sky, sifting for shrimp, you try
to keep count: no little ones lost in the
creek or sneaking away to the hunting.
What you need's eyes in the back of your head.

II

Like two voices shifting into pitch, our
coastline after four thousand years maps yours.
Your fen and creek are gone, you wouldn't know
this fine sand drifted with pines; but here are
your mud-flats, become lithographic, and
here your people: four-toes, twisted, no use
at the hunt; this girl, months-heavy, inching
her way, clawed feet curled hard into the mud;
and the children, quick, unhurried, knowing
themselves alone possessed of the future.

# Estuarine

In the clear grace of dream I stood
high on the Edge, the wind tugging, the world
tumbling far below. Tiny lights signed
across the valleys and I knew,
if I dived, the icy sky would bear me

but I awoke at sea level, estuarine
and silted, caught seven years
at slack water, waiting
a turn of the tide.

# Shavuot

Under the cherry-
trees you sit,
drifted in white:

glass–maker's
daughter. Not
my place to

dream of you
with child, your
fine–spun

bones singing
like ice on ice.
Waiting a touch

upon the wrist
you sit, drifted
in white: a promise

made between the
flowering cherry and
the Feast of Weeks.

# Cockleshells

We are walking the littoral
of October, watching the tide

reach its decision. I carry
merely yesterday's meanings but

you are already translated, turning
towards the bright months while I

collect October's cockleshells,
curetted cleanly by the sea.

# Poem for Sabine

It must have been Hamburg: the dream didn't say.
Dark shapes shadowed the water:
we were run aground, out in the roads.
On the quay you waited with the unsaid word,
*Krebs*, the crab, the unforgiving.

I woke to the rain-sound, stranded in August,
remembering the valley's steeps, your long
and lovely hair. Schreib mir! –
this sheaved air hints at winterings,
the sea's way wide between us.

# Magnolia

*for Linda*

But so soon, this first
drifting of bravura pink
back to the earth.
Leaves April still
so young. Still
so green.

# Among Alphabets

We met among alphabets. I saw myself
Greek: walking the walls,
inviolate as logic, mistress
of philosophy's glassy tongue.
Translation came slow. I learned to trust
Hebrew's rich misreadings, risk breeding
between the lines: language of faith,
our leap in the dark.

# Fox-Seers

Your body the decision
of an instant and a

sine-wave's flow from
hedge to hedge, your

moment's stare uncoloured by
our headlights' white and we

are become merely (*kuck mal,
Fuchs!*) fox-seers.

# Autumn Child

*for Patrick*


Autumn child
you would be born with the leaf-fall
the catch in the air
that tells the year's turn

tonight, a rag of cloud
blindfolding the face of the moon

am I leaving you
or moving to greet you?

II

# Missel-Child

The lady of the moon is in travail,
her white face waxen as the missel-fruit.

The gravelled path gives way to broken angles,
burials of water. Follow it.

Creep into the hospice of the yew,
its pale lying-place. Curl up there. Wait.

# Unadopted

When you lift the receiver the story
is already unfolding: quiet
insistent cross-talk of

a party line. Behind the lock-ups
June hangs heavy,
deep sea-green and sour

on the tongue. Wires hum
along the cutting. At the edge
of the permissible you finger-

spell the word: *unadopted*. Radios
talk of Rhodesia, and at night
the fitful banging of the trap.

# Funeral and Fox

## I

Good Friday began in New York, watching
the parade from tall windows: stiltwalkers,
a school of small witches. I had to kill
the badman to get the girl, went out to
the forest cabin to see the hoods and
hire a gun. No way, they said, you'll never
take him. Back with the witches, I told the
children: See, if you die famous, this is
the send-off you'll get.

## II

Later, in the village house, I met him
in the airing cupboard, his burnt umber
face trained on me from his foxhole among
the bedsheets. There was shit on the patterned
green lino, the towels in disarray. O
I know you, I said, you're the word this house
will never hear. He fired past me, watched as
I fumbled the key; lit out to the woods
beyond the garden.

# At the Castle

A four-square block of wood tapering from 5 in. to 3 in.
A grate of oak stanchions set diagonally
A portcullis, the chase of which may still be seen

All angles are of brick

And carved ornament in head and jambs
And only the excellence of the mortar
And the soile betwene the waulles grue ful of elders

But little of them exists beyond the broken wall-ends
But the patterns in black brick are simpler
But this is only conjecture

By what must have been a miscalculation of levels
Circa factorum le murther holles de novo
Much of the brickwork having fallen away

Of fireplaces, and the toothings on the west tower
Of payments to men watching in the moat at night
Of the machicolations, and probably the slabs

On the right-hand turret the maunch or sleeve
Pro levelyng le erthe intra muros
The burning of the bricks

Then felle alle the castelle to ruine

# Water, its Voicings

Night excavates, reopens
old coursings. In the mouth of

the culvert language grew, green
and forbidden, fingering

the edges of thought (*we have
a little sister, she has*

*no breasts*), knuckling deep into
brickwork, the secret places

of walls. Persuasive, night pries
through shut springs, sealed fountains:

complicit, you open your
throat to water, its voicings.

# Katherine

Katherine has been dead a week

                    I think of her in this way
                    off & on − that strange
                    ghost, with the eyes far
                    apart, & the drawn mouth

the feel of her

                    dragging herself across her
                    room

a Japanese doll

                    putting on a white wreath,
                    & leaving us, called away;
                    made dignified, chosen.
                    And then one pitied her

in a room high up
childlikeness somewhere

                    felt her reluctant to wear
                    that wreath, which was an
                    ice cold one. And she was
                    only 33

posed & twisted

& the doll on the bed, which I detest


Katherine has been dead a week

                    visual impressions kept
                    coming & coming before
                    me

strange ghost, with the eyes far apart

                    very tidy, bright, &
                    somehow like a dolls
                    house

& the drawn mouth

kept coming & coming
and I was jealous

                                    And I was jealous of her
                                    writing – the only writing
                                    I have ever been jealous of

we met, beyond death
in a room high up

                                    that faint ghost, with the
                                    steady eyes, the mocking
                                    lips, &, at the end, the
                                    wreath set on her hair

the mocking lips
& the feel of her
& the doll on the bed, which I detest


Katherine has been dead a week

                                    how we met, beyond
                                    death, & shook hands;
                                    saying something by way
                                    of explanation, &
                                    friendship: yet I knew she
                                    was dead

Japanese doll

kept coming & coming
and I was jealous

childlikeness somewhere

                                    agonised, & at moments
                                    that direct flick at the
                                    thing seen which was her
                                    gift

dragging herself across her room
something driven & forced
yet I knew she was dead

                                    & the perpetual rather
                                    sordid worries & gibes

& the feel of her
& the feel of her

& something driven &
forced to cram into one
year the growth of five or
six

& the doll on the bed, which I detest


Katherine has been dead a week

husky & feeble, crawling
about the room like a little
old woman

the drawn mouth
something driven & forced


had her look of a Japanese
doll, with the fringe
combed quite straight
across her forehead

kept coming & coming
yet I knew she was dead

and I

a kind of childlikeness
somewhere which has
been much disfigured

& the doll

that strange ghost

posed & twisted


Katherine has been dead a week

I think of her in this way
off & on −

the feel of her

& somehow like a dolls
house

yet I knew
yet I knew

explanation, & friendship:
yet I knew she was dead

and I

          and I was jealous of her
          writing

the doll

the mocking lips

          dragging herself across her
          room

& the feel of her

& the doll

          that strange ghost

& the doll

          the mocking lips

& the doll on the bed, which I detest

# In a Richer Mine

By Parma, on the flood-plain. The river,
in spate, dragging ochre under dirty

nails. Submerged a child, you resurface a
doll: mechanical eyelids, face cauled &

streaked with slip. Thin cries from the attic, zinc
disc in the spine: *within this room she is,*

*whose eyes I caused to be put out, but kept*
*alive.* Mama, mama! In the village

the Scouse priest relishes his chthonic words,
smacking his chops as you, the five-months' child,

awake and clutch under my heart, digging
with half-formed fingers in a richer mine.

# Shilling Visit

Night bares her mossy teeth in welcome, indicates
the parlour, wherein lies her knock-kneed daughter
Moon, scratching the thinnest of thin livings

amid the hoarded three-piece suites. The priest
rattles his box of knucklebones and nods
towards the back-room, where lolls Impudence

against the faience, gilled girl dragged to air,
the silver hook of *monsieur l'accoucheur*
a pretty pendant to her lower lip.

      ★

Fall of a coin. Your shilling in the slot.
Obsequious gaslit smiles. *Hony soyt.*

# Cedar

## I

This cedar is an old god. The woman
mistrusts it. Look, she says, my breasts
are empty. There is nothing
in this month but moon.

## II

She runs her thumb along the teeth
of the lily, seven days in flower after
seven secret years; and now the hag-mouth
of the seedpod.

## III

Hulled in sleep, the woman dreams of ships,
of knives and pyres: matters known
to cedar, the old god. Moon hangs
in the roof-trees. No intercessor.

## Among the Gods (Persephone)

Who is the god, not of gardens but of
their edge-lands? O, give over,
Priapos, we all know about *you*, creeping up

on the lovely Lotis, looking
to give her one to remember you
by, but a couple of brays

from some dumb ass and you've lost the plot
and your hard-on, the nymphette
scarpered. – No, this is a subtler god,

he of the poison-fingers,
*digitalis purpurea*, spiring the
shady places past the orchard,

pink bells mottled with platelets, some pretty
disease, and each white blotch with
its own pinprick fever-spot. – A better

seducer than you, Priapos,
he knows the lovely lady belladonna,
anemone, crocus, small

and secret wings of cyclamen – and yes,
of course, the orchid. He's the one
who slips the ice-bright seed between my lips

and with it comes the knowledge
I was always, always his.

III

# Male Nude by R.B. Kitaj

His flank, its hollows
and solidities: ribcage,
belly, cock. His arm
upraised: the patch
of dark, its echo beneath
charcoal trace of hip-
bone.
      Not standing-for but
standing, simply: what
then is it to be thus, plain-
spoken, in possession,
undisputed?

# Mono

A race-horse that runs single
Absolute rule
In one way only
A monk

A hunt of one day
Fixed, steadfast, constant
Walking alone
Marrying one wife

One-fingered
One-eyed
Of unvaried sound
One-toothed

Plucked from one stem
Carved from one block
Of one kind
Simple

A single horse
One-horned
With one mourner
A bed for one only
A coffin

To sleep alone
With but one sandal
With but one limb
With but one room
Consisting of one clause

Left alone by one's mother
In a single night
Having but one child
With but one sole

Left without a robe
Digging with one point
Eating but once in the day

Wielding the sceptre alone
Dealing with monosyllables
At a solitary board

Watching alone
Single in one's opinion
Of simple nature
A song sung alone.

# Portrait of a Young Woman

This morning, the moon's volte-face as
the month changed handedness, the right

profile sharp against sky, the left
dissolving in shadow at nape

and jawline – gestures rehearsed by
Leonardo contemplating

surface and stylus, movements of
hand and mind this unknown face makes

legible, its sweeps of grace and
energy always from rightward

edge extending infinitely
into leftward space, structuring

a grammar shared through this half-month,
etched in this new moon's metalpoint.

# With Joe on Silver Street

*Tuesday 1 August 1967*
*Said goodbye to Kenneth this morning. He seemed odd. On the spur of the*
*moment I asked if he wanted to come home to Leicester with me. He looked*
*surprised and said, 'No.'*

– from the diary of Joe Orton

In scratty fake-fur jackets, jaunty caps
and baseball boots we saunter Silver Street,
skiving our *l*s: it's *Siuv*er Street to slack-
mouthed Midlanders like us, who can't be arsed
with alveolar laterals. Of course,
RADA and elocution did the trick,
but still you keep a hint of Saffron Lane –
it charms the pants off Peggy and the rest,
just like the coat: 'Cheap clothes suit me,' you smirked,
'It's cos I'm from the gutter'; and it works,
they're all down on their knees, lapping it up.
Sometimes I think I hate you, Joe: I can
be cruel, but cruelty is something pure
for you, a fire that kills and makes things clean
and true; and I know anger, but the rage
that shoots your star high through the London nights
is something I'm afraid to face. You've travelled
far beyond me, Joe, and you don't plan
on coming back, I know; but here we are
on Silver Street, and look, in black and white,
that little word you never had the time
to strike out from those last blind lines, Joe: *home.*

# Der Tod in Venedig

All nights are white and silk the heaviest
caress. Your little god lacks language, strains
to unleash speech's miscegenate flood –

★

The barber's sycophantic fingers on
your lip, your cheek. A katabasis you
endure through rouged and painted dreams: *My art,*

*signor, will give you youth* (a wink, a glint
of sharp small teeth), *will let you taste again*
*of love.* A dish of soft and splitting fruit –

★

Noon is a burning-glass: blind light on water,
vitrifying air shaped to a name, a call.
A white arm beckons seawards, and you fall.

# The Hardened Criminals of Tomorrow

Which was funny, because he couldn't
get it up: crashed and burned, he
told me, crashed
and burned. We sat in his Merc by
the reservoir chopping up
*Cosmo*. Take me, I said, I'm
yours, because –

Of course you have to catch them young enough.

# When I was quite small I would sometimes dream

All the perceptions of the human mind resolve themselves
in her last picture the camera had lingered at the hip
she's sweet, isn't she? just look at that

I hope you will be ready to own publicly
it was about eleven o'clock in the morning, mid October
Weidmann appeared before you in a five o'clock edition

They say when trouble comes close ranks, and so
the town itself is dreary; not much is there except
I mind as if it were yesterday my first sight

Sometimes the Alps lying below in the moonlight
the rowdy gang of singers who sat at the scattered tables
when I was quite small I would sometimes dream

# Miss Yamada Has Gotten Married

## A Romance

I
Miss Yamada returned home from abroad yesterday.

II
The stars are pretty tonight. The cat is stalking a mouse. I have
resolved to quit smoking from today on. One shouldn't waste
even a penny.

III
I bought this book because Miss Yamada kept on
recommending it to me. I have gotten into the habit of staying
up late at night. Next month I will move near to the university.

My future plan is to become a doctor. I think I would have
become a volleyball player if I had been a little taller.

IV
My third younger sister will be fifteen years old this year. The
young people of the village have all gone away into the military.

This is the age of science. Recently, all households have come to
use fluorescent lights. The government of this country is taking a
hard line on foreign imports. The morning trains are
unimaginably crowded.

V
I ate *sashimi* yesterday. Tanaka never showed up for his
appointment with me. I decided to repaint the walls as I don't
like the present color.

VI
When I was small my mother often read to me from the Bible.
The number of living creatures on earth is beyond count. Cats
can see even at night. When autumn comes one hears the sound
of many insects.

My father used to sing when he drank *sake*. He said his farewell with tears in his eyes. If only the doctor had come sooner, my father's life could have been saved.

VII
The grounds of a shrine are always nicely swept. One mustn't do anything against the rules.

VIII
Tanaka is all talk and no action. 'I want to take a trip somewhere with good scenery. I intend to save my money and buy a tape-recorder. My future plans are to work for the public good. Let's all build strong constitutions by participating in sport!'

Tanaka has recently built a house. I hear that he knows French. He makes radios all day without even eating. Tanaka's wife is a person of firm character. She always has on slacks.

IX
There are peoples in the world without any written language.

X
It seems that Miss Yamada is going to the United States next month. The winters are very cold here. You can see the mountains from my apartment.

The fish store man is always in good spirits. Somehow I just can't like that sort of person. I would like to leave the world behind and go live alone in the mountains.

XI
My grandfather told me about past times. 'Once upon a time there was an old man and an old woman. Free soap was distributed to five hundred persons. The snow fell to a depth of one meter. Humanity succeeded in going to the moon.'

XII
Tanaka finally showed up when the party was almost over.

It started to rain just as I was leaving the house. My mother called to me as I was walking in the garden. 'Did you hear the news? Miss Yamada has gotten married!' There was a throng of people gathered in the plaza. The ship was approaching.

## XIII
The fine weather has continued for a month now. In a few days this year will draw to its close.

## XIV
I parted from Miss Yamada in front of the station, saying '*Sayōnara*.' Love makes people beautiful.

I'm going to heat some water and fix green tea. The children are waving flags. There is nothing to eat.

# America

Broad and smiling as a Sunday
rivermouth, impossible word

between us: *america*. Wide
and easy speech, argument smooth

and seamless as an egg. Half-tongued
I stumble through the station at

Stephansplatz, past memorials
to lost wars, and to the playground

in the beautiful gardens, where
I watch my children disappear

undisturbed: macht nichts, sie kommen
wieder zurück. America

is where we can never meet, though
we lived there together for years.

# A long war, and now the returning

A long war, and now the returning. The low white buildings
of the small town's railway station. Bright summer flowers in

hanging baskets, and the name of the town picked out in white
stones on the embankment, though what that name is you cannot

say. The trains have arrived and are standing, hissing, at the
platforms. (There is sound, certainly, but no dialogue.) The

returning ones disembark from the trains and begin to drift
along the platforms towards those who have apparently

gathered to meet them. Neither group shows any sign of haste
or excitement. The returning ones walk shufflingly, heads

bowed. The waiting ones regard them without recognition
or concern. In fact, the two groups are of no interest to

each other: the ones who wait have long grown accustomed to
waiting, and the ones who return are in any case dead.

IV

# Fosse Way

To-day was once Britain.

Acres begin with running north-west.
There were forks and running due north.
Rich wool. Properly a large town.
Unusually quiet.
The sower guides the wheels.
Square words from the charms.

Start out on the line with turns due north.
It bears once more the fosse before
the town through it. Hardly praised.
The land the views a very stone.
Golden sun.

Trees are not luxuriant exactly.
For the country climbing gradually to higher ground.
Sometimes a small down.

The villa at the rich weeks in the way nowadays.
Exactly they were practically Britons.

There are not hundreds south-east of the line.
These rivers beyond were mines practically.
Beyond completely followed.

The richer Britons themselves better had been born.
Comes into conquest were many.
The life. Perhaps they were as many
as twenty in some extremely.

Built of timber only once.
Traces of a staircase glass tessellated.
Painted by means of the heat led
underneath the walls.
The poorest were a good deal more than our own.

Usually cold.

# Hollow Meadows

*Hollow, hull* (of ships and plants), κοῖλος, *skull* (as κεφαλὴ and *caput* that which holds, contains), *hole, hold,* etc. *Hell.*
– Gerard Manley Hopkins, diary, 1863

Corridor-coloured. A place
of eyes. Things
put away,    privily

★

englishedith
08-05-2005, 16:07
:help: Can anyone tell me is this place still there and what was it home/hospital/institution?

PhilipB
08-05-2005, 19:33
As far as I'm aware this used to be a Borstel. The building is still there but not used as such now.

deecee
08-05-2005, 22:51
A friend of ours had a son who used to stay there because of very bad epilepsy, this was back in the 70s. It was a kind of institution for people with mental and physical disabilities.

★

Chlorine is heavy, creeps
like nightwatchmen. Clocks
mock:  tonic /
            clonic /

★

HughW
09-05-2005, 21:38
Three possible manifestations of the same institution?!

from Pawson & Brailsford's *Illustrated Guide to Sheffield* 1862:

In 1849 the Guardians leased from the Duke of Norfolk about 50 acres of moorland, at Hollow Meadows, about six miles from the town, with a view of reclaiming it by pauper labour. Nearly the whole of the land has been brought under cultivation, and sub-let to farm tenants. The Farm, as it is called, is still retained by the Guardians, and a number of the able-bodied men who require relief in times of bad trade are sent to labour at it. The undertaking has been so successful that at the time we write (February 1862) the Guardians are in negotiation for the leasing of further land.

from *White's Directory* 1901:

The Truant School, at Hollow Meadows, was established in 1879 as a means of discipline for recalcitrant children, and will hold 90 boys.

from *White's Directory* 1919/20:

The Sheffield Educational Committee Industrial School is at Hollow Meadows, about seven miles from the City, on the main road to Manchester, and provides for 90 boys, the average number of inmates being about 80. The boys are largely employed in market-gardening. Superintendent, Mr Isaac McHardy.

★

Walking stammers, unsequenced with
stagefright: requires a trick, a sleight
of mind – *look, over there, quick* – Ha!
Fooled you. Faster. Too fast. Feste, the
jester, harries & grips – *O lente lente*
*currite* –

★

Ousetunes
10–05–2005, 07:23
I think I can remember, when in the 1970s we seemed to go
over the Snake Pass nearly every Sunday, my mum referring to
the place as a 'Bad Boys Home' or a 'Naughty Boys School'.
Something like that.

★

The baby. Starfish
mouths behind
glass cross-
examined by steel
threads. Air
gelid, thick like
brine. Is he
dead, is he
mine? Mouths
open anemone-
red but I
am far inside
green, soundless,
unfathomed

★

Jan39
25–05–2005, 20:20
I was told it was last used as an isolation hospital.

★

They should have left the moon alone. I saw it
this morning still high in the west, looking
so pure and alone but it isn't, not
any more. Not after that Sunday night,
or Monday I suppose, it was four in
the morning but I couldn't sleep because
of the heartburn and his elbow, it must
have been, jammed under my ribs. You couldn't

tell what anything was at first, and the voices
all broken and fuzzing like off-station
radio; and that place so utterly
empty. They should have left the moon alone.

★

Stoner
30-05-2005, 10:36
At the back of the site is a private woodland that you can still
walk through. I remember as a youngster walking through the
wood and looking into the hospital which specialised in fitting
artificial limbs. From the woods you could see into a room
which contained a huge stock of spare limbs which was very
spooky to look at as a child.

★

Superconductive. Tripping &
lapping. Above the weir's
furred lip, the pools rusty
with sunlight, chuckling like
uncles: *Tha' better behave or tha'llt
g' t't Meadows.* Over the moor
the swifts are screaming: *news
news* —

★

OntarioOwl
25-01-2006, 03:06
When we were naughty as kids our grandparents used to
threaten us with being sent to the 'naughty boys' home at
Rivelin.

★

I must have been about seven, my brother was still a baby,
sleeping in the cot in my parents' room, and I had the little back
bedroom which looked out over the allotments. The storm

woke me. I crawled to the end of the bed and pulled the
curtains open to watch. The sky was pale green and the thunder
didn't just roll like drums, it cracked like a whip, like someone
splitting the world in two. She was standing just by the shed,
over the way. She was wearing a long white dress and she held
her hands to her ears as though the noise hurt her, and she kept
shaking her head as if she was saying *No, no* to someone I
couldn't see. The lightning flashed like an x-ray and she looked
up and she looked right at me and I saw her face, she looked
more frightened than anyone I had ever seen and she started
trying to tell me something, but I couldn't hear for the rain and
the thunder and the shut window, and I heard the baby start to
cry and my mam and dad waking up, and then something
moved behind me and I turned and it was the cat, she must have
been scared by the storm and got out of the kitchen and up the
stairs, and when I looked back out of the window she was gone,
the lady was gone and I never saw her again.

# Persephone in Adiyaman

Carious, she breaks surface. Spitting earth-
seeds, she wants to show you her new science,

ground-breaking initiatives in the field
of alveolar exchange – efficient

adaptation to be sure, but she was
always a quick learner; even, some said,

precocious. Proud earth-breather, she tries to
describe her fast-track evolution but

her words clot, baffled by the loam that fills
her mouth. For the first time, doubt registers:

can it be she is mistaken, must she
after all breathe air? Flowerlike, her

lungs expand just once. The silence of the
whole earth screams inside the caves of her ears.

## Philadelphus

Lovely philadelphus, torn by today's
unthinking rain, yours is the sorrow of
summer brides, your wedding of white and green
like theirs so swift, so swiftly lost to time.

# Rheidol Valley

Within a semicircle on the isolated hill.
By the seashore between the estuaries.
The monument. Excavated. Defended.
A high bank with stone ramparts and ditches.
The natural slope of the ground. The entrance.

To the south-east, and at each corner holes. Into the solid rock.
Great posts to hold the gates, strengthen the turn of the wall.
The stone facing. Along the inside of the wall. Close against two sides.
Solitary.

In the extreme south-east there is no sign.
They continued to live their old lives. A straighter line over the hill.
Often very beautiful. Cut out of the solid rock.

Above Taliesin foxgloves and wild roses. It is not known.
The remains of a causeway. Three miles upstream from the north.
Almost hidden by moss. Straight on through a pinewood. Much
        more luminous.

A steep climb. A lovely way up. Yellow gorse and young green bracken.
Half an acre of bluebells like a sheet of water.
The real way is uncertain again.

Obvious once you know where to look. The lower hillside track.
Copper mines. The precipices. Flat green meadows. The abbey.
Sometimes fringed with yellow irises.
Pale green on the black of its surface.

# Priest

(John Singer Sargent, *Vespers*, 1909)


This priest makes no demand, merely watches
from the shadow of the colonnade.
He is a gesture: his dark substance indicates
by contrast the white uneven path
and whiter wall of (we may suppose)
his church. Balanced
by the solid dark of cypresses beyond
the path and shallow flight
of white stone steps, broken walls
scrambled by mimosa, he absorbs
all ratiocination. Grace
is the dark soft cloak he wears.

# Heron

The slow beat of wings and your cry, harsh through the dark, Pallas'
sign to the Greeks who crawled the plain in the night's third watch, spies

from the ships – your cry it was announced you, that same birth-cry
torn from your throat in Egypt as you rose, shining, over

the delta: world-bringer, soul of the sun. Yet today in
the rain you define silence, are instinct with it, watcher

at the water's edge, compelling in stillness and telic
utterly. No messenger, you bear no meaning: our creed

of augurs and annunciations remains ours alone.

# In the dying days of the year we walked

*…River with sea*
*shall mingle its stream…*


In the dying days of the year we walked
by the river and wondered at the meeting of
salt water and sweet as the tide swung like
the weighing of day against night. The river
opened its hands to the sea and cast no look
back to its high days rilling over the shale
and did not mourn its course fixed first by the
rocks' blind science and then by the minds
of men. We walked by the river and weighed
our small works as the year swung and
turned like the tide in its saltsweet dying days.

# Secret Name

*for Rowan*


In winter's dark you are dual:
we cannot know you.
Through festivals of souls and light
you keep your secret

and when spring's storms wake
the earth's dark calm to violent life

you will come
to claim your name.

# Climbing the Hill at Sunset

*...before I had always taken the sunset and the sun as quite out of gauge with
each other... but today I inscaped them together and made the sun the true eye
and ace of the whole, as it is.*

– Gerard Manley Hopkins, *Journal*

We climbed past St Rhuddlad's
to Pen-y-Foel, the hill
not bare though but
rich with small lives.
Rabbits ran from your
high child voices, while
tiny wings creaked
and beat around us.
England lay blank
beyond the slate hills,
the world curving
into the west; and the sun,
true eye and ace,
commanded all.

# Notes

'At the Castle'
The text is taken from a Department of the Environment pamphlet on Kirby Muxloe Castle, Leicestershire (HMSO, 1957).

'Katherine'
The text is taken from various entries in Virginia Woolf's diaries (published in five volumes by Penguin); the subject is Katherine Mansfield.

'Mono'
The text is taken from Liddell & Scott's *Greek–English Lexicon*.

'When I was quite small I would sometimes dream'
The text comprises the first lines of various novels.

'Miss Yamada Has Gotten Married'
The text is taken from the *Oxford Basic Japanese–English Dictionary*.

'Fosse Way' and 'Rheidol Valley'
The text is taken from G.M. Boumphrey, *Along the Roman Roads* (George Allen & Unwin, 1935).

'Hollow Meadows'
Hollow Meadows is a hamlet on the A57 just outside Sheffield. It is the site of a former hospital or institution. Parts of the text are taken from an online discussion at www.sheffieldforum.co.uk/archive/index.php/t-39533.html.

'Persephone in Adiyaman'
Based on a report in the *Guardian* (4 February 2010): 'Turkish police have recovered the body of a 16-year-old girl they say was buried alive by relatives in an "honour" killing carried out as punishment for talking to boys. The girl, who has been identified only by the initials MM, was found in a sitting position with her hands tied, in a two-metre hole dug under a chicken pen outside her home in Kahta, in the south-eastern province of Adiyaman.'